CROYDON
TO
EAST
GRINSTEAD

Vic Mitchell and Keith Smith

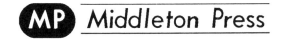

The route south of Oxted was included in our *Branch Lines to East Grinstead* in 1984. It is covered again herein as the line has changed greatly in the intervening years and also many interesting historic photographs have come to light in that period. A fresh presentation of this section has therefore been possible.

Cover picture: LMS-designed and Brighton-built 2-6-4T no. 42105 hauls the 5.20pm London Bridge to Tunbridge Wells West through the two non-electrified platforms at Selsdon on 28th August 1951. Electric trains used the other two until 1983. (R.C.Riley)

First published March 1995

ISBN 1 873793 48 0

© *Middleton Press 1995*

Design - Deborah Goodridge

Published by Middleton Press
Easebourne Lane
Midhurst
West Sussex
GU29 9AZ
Tel: 01730 813169

Printed & bound by Biddles Ltd,
Guildford and Kings Lynn

CONTENTS

ACKNOWLEDGEMENTS

We have received assistance from many of the photographers credited in the captions and for this we are very grateful. We would also like to express our gratitude to P.G.Barnes, J.F.Bradshaw, R.M.Casserley, G.Croughton, J.N.Faulkner, J.B.Horne, F.Hornby, A.Ll.Lambert, N.Langridge, Mrs M.Mason, D.Monk-Steel, D.L.Smith, A.Neale, Mr.D. & Dr.S.Salter, D.Wallis, G.Weaver, C.Wilson and our supportive wives.

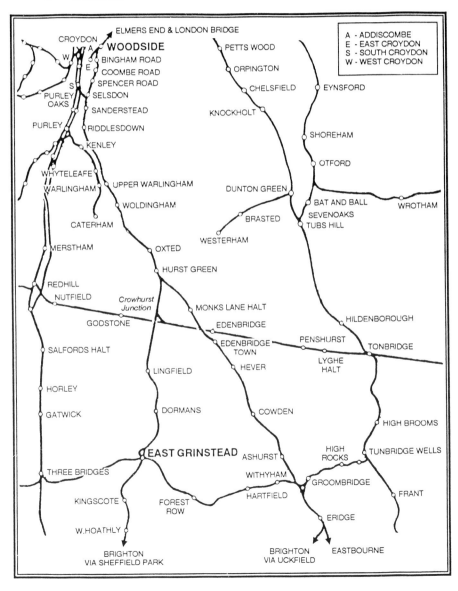

GEOGRAPHICAL SETTING

Croydon is situated on the foot of the dip slope of the North Downs. The route rises on the Chalk of this structure, descending through Oxted Tunnel and down the scarp slope from which this material was once extensively quarried.

On the approach to Oxted the line traverses narrow outcrops of Gault Clay and Folkestone Beds. From Hurst Green to Lingfield the route descends into the Eden Valley where the tracks are on Wealden Clay, once of economic importance for brick production.

Most of the remainder of the journey involves a steady climb to East Grinstead on the sands of the Tunbridge Wells Beds.

All maps are to the scale of 25" to 1 mile, unless otherwise indicated.

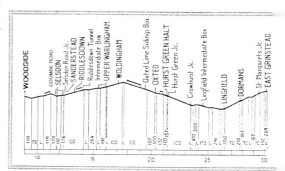

HISTORICAL BACKGROUND

The early 1840s saw the completion of the London to Brighton line which was operated by the London, Brighton & South Coast Railway. Also finished at that time was the South Eastern Railway's route between London and Dover which branched from the London to Brighton at Redhill. The company's preferred route via Oxted was denied it by politicians who then (as now) thought they knew best how to run railways and believed that only one line was required south of London.

The Surrey & Sussex Junction Railway was formed in 1864 (with LBSCR backing) to build a line from South Croydon to the Tunbridge Wells - Uckfield route via Oxted. Much of the civil engineering, including Oxted Tunnel, was completed before the company collapsed in 1866. Some track was laid in the Selsdon area but this was abandoned and became over-grown.

The LBSCR opened a branch from Three Bridges to East Grinstead on 9th July 1855 and extended operations to Tunbridge Wells on 1st October 1866.

An Act for the Croydon, Oxted & East Grinstead Railway was passed in 1878. North of the original SER main line it was jointly owned by the LBSCR and the SER; south thereof it was LBSCR property. The line was opened on 10th March 1884.

In the meantime the Lewes & East Grinstead Railway had opened on 1st August 1882, the combined lines giving the LBSCR an alternative route between London and Brighton. The joint line gave the SER direct access to its Edenbridge - Tonbridge line and avoided the use of the London - Brighton main line. The connecting spur was at Crowhurst Junction.

The Woodside and South Croydon Railway was another SER/LBSCR joint venture. This received its Act on 6th August 1880 and was opened on 10th August 1885. It provided a link between the SER's 1864 "Mid-Kent" line to Croydon (Addiscombe Road) and Selsdon Road, on the joint line. The line gave the SER access to other parts of its system, although it was used infrequently by long-distance trains.

The railway map of the area was completed on 1st October 1888 when the Oxted & Groombridge Railway was opened. It ran south-east from Hurst Green and was operated by the LBSCR. (Services south to Edenbridge Town commenced on 1st January of that year).

The Woodside-Selsdon (Road) section was closed to regular passenger services from 1st January 1917 until 30th September 1935, when electrification took place. (Electric services ran south as far as Sanderstead.) It was completely closed as a through route on 13th May 1983.

All the lines of the district became part of the Southern Railway on 1st January 1923 and part of the Southern Region of British Railways upon nationalisation in 1948.

Closures of associated lines took place on 16th March 1958 (East Grinstead to Lewes) and 1st January 1967 (Three Bridges to Tunbridge Wells).

On 18th June 1962, the first of nineteen 3-car Diesel Electric Multiple Units were introduced. From 5th October 1987, all trains were electrically operated to East Grinstead but a few DEMUs serving the Uckfield line continued to work north of Oxted, mainly in the peak hours.

PASSENGER SERVICES

Woodside to Selsdon

There were 10 or 11 trains each way from the opening until 1901 but by 1914 this had increased to 21. Most were operated by steam railmotors running between Woodside and Selsdon Road only, but some journeys were extended north to Lewisham Junction. The August 1914 timetable showed only three trains, these all originating at Tonbridge and running to London Bridge. Services ceased on 15th March 1915 and the line was officially closed to passengers in 1917. No regular Sunday services were operated. During the closure period, some excursions used the line, notably New Cross - Brighton day trip trains.

Electrification upon reopening in 1935 brought the lavish provision of a 30-minute interval service, seven days a week, between Charing Cross and Sanderstead. World War II necessitated reductions which continued over the years until the cessation of services in 1983, when there were trains in peak hours on Mondays to Fridays only, between Elmers End and Sanderstead.

Selsdon to East Grinstead

The table below gives an outline of the development of train services from London. Most of the trains under the heading "To Oxted" continued to Edenbridge (Town) or beyond (notably Tunbridge Wells), while many of those listed "To East Grinstead" ran on to Lewes and Brighton or Tunbridge Wells via Forest Row.

| | To Oxted | | To East Grinstead | |
	Weekdays	Sundays	Weekdays	Sundays
1885	4	3	4	2
1901	10	5	10	2
1915	12	5	14	2
1930	20	6	16	3
1950	11	4	16	5

A timetable revolution took place in 1955 when an hourly service from Victoria to Tunbridge Wells West via East Grinstead was introduced, a connection at Oxted being provided for the Edenbridge Town route. A basic hourly timetable was maintained throughout the DEMU era and a more useful half-hourly interval service was introduced with electric traction in 1987. The evening and Sunday service continued to be hourly.

Destinations of down weekday departures from Oxted		
	1934	1954
Tunbridge Wells W. via Edenbridge Town	13	15
Tunbridge Wells W. via East Grinstead	4	7
East Grinstead only	4	3
Brighton via Uckfield	2	3
Brighton via Sheffield Park	4	3
Brighton via Haywards Heath	2	1
Brighton via Eridge	1	1
Eastbourne via Eridge	2	2
Cowden only	1	0
Lewes only	1	0
Forest Row only	1	1
Some Eastbourne trains were a part of Brighton trains as far as Eridge, where they divided.		

WOODSIDE

The 1911 revision at 6" to 1 mile has the line from Elmers End at the top and that to Croydon (Addiscombe Road) on the left. Bingham Road is shown on this page but the halt of that name is inexplicably not marked. The route continues from the bottom of this page to the top right of the next one, on which is shown Coombe Lane Station, Spencer Road Halt and Selsdon Road Station. Top left is East Croydon Station and Central Croydon Goods Depot.

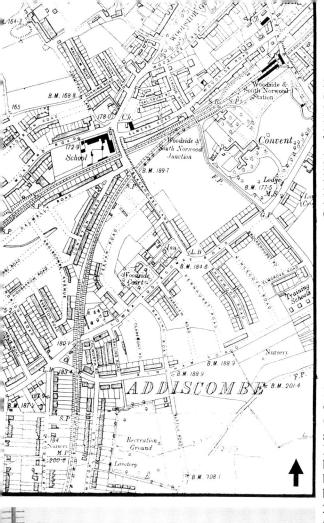

1. The SER's branch from Lewisham was completed south of Beckenham to Croydon (Addiscombe Road) on 1st April 1864 but a station was not opened at Woodside until 1871. It was built to serve Croydon Racecourse. It became a junction on 10th August 1885 and a bay platform was provided, one of its rails being visible to the right of H class 0-4-4T no. 279, which is bound for Selsdon Road. (J.B.Gent coll.)

The 1912 map has the line from Elmers End on the right and the Selsdon route below the Addiscombe line on the left.

2. The bay line had been to the left of the perforated concrete signal post shown in this photograph taken in November 1948. The station was named "Woodside & South Norwood" between 1st October 1908 and 2nd October 1944. The signal box was built in 1877 and the coal siding (right) was laid in the following year. (D.Clayton)

3. The signal is set for the Addiscombe route as a down train departs on 16th October 1955. The goods yard closed on 30th September 1963 and the platforms were extended towards us later. The signal box was in use until 24th June 1984. (Pamlin Prints)

4. The main building spanned the tracks; its west elevation is visible in picture no. 1. Also featured is a Jowett Javelin which soon became part of transport history. (J.B.Gent coll.)

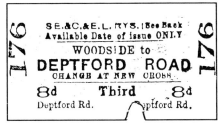

Other views of this station and junction are to be found in the companion album
London Bridge to Addiscombe.

5. This photograph was taken on 12th May 1983 from the bridge seen in picture no. 2, as 2EPB no. 5746 worked the 16.52 Sanderstead to Elmers End service. The junction was closed four days later, although the last trains ran on Friday the 13th. (D.Gould)

6. Woodside down platform is in the distance and the site of the Selsdon line on the right as a railtour passes by on 15th May 1993. Very few have visited Addiscombe - this one set out at 05.00 from Carnforth with Windsor & Eton Riverside as its destination. No. 33023 is hauling maroon painted coaches and is seen from Blackhorse Lane bridge. (B.Morrison)

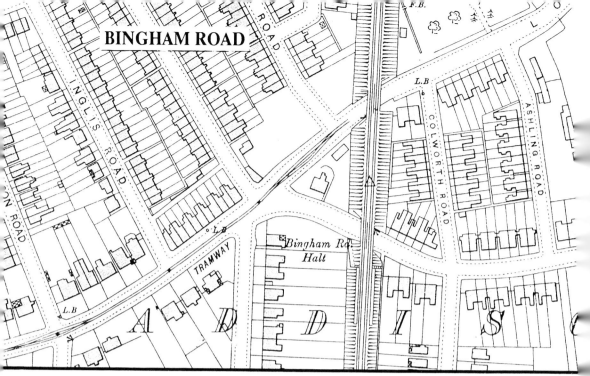

BINGHAM ROAD

Bingham Rd. Halt

The 1910 map indicates the location of the halt, so designated from its opening on 1st September 1906 until its first closure on 15th March 1915. Also marked is the tramway terminus which is illustrated in *Croydon's Tramways* (Middleton Press).

7. Reopened as a station on 30th September 1935, two new entrances with covered stairways were provided. Those to the up platform are behind the Hillman (right) and those to the down side are beyond the Wolseley behind it. (R.K.Kirkland)

8. With paint peeling, the SR standard canopies were shortly to become redundant after being recorded on 6th May 1983. The last train on the 13th was the 19.30 from Sanderstead. (J.Scrace)

BRITISH RAILWAYS (S)
This ticket is issued subject to the Bye-laws,
Regulations and Conditions contained in the
Publications and Notices of and applicable to the
Railway Executive.
Bingham Road to
CANNON STREET or WATERLOO
Via Woodside
Third Class. Fare 10½d. H
NOT TRANSFERABLE

BRITISH RAILWAYS (S)
This ticket is issued subject to the Bye-laws,
Regulations and Conditions contained in the
Publications and Notices of and applicable to the
Railway Executive.
Bingham Road to
Bingham Rd.   Bingham Rd.
Cannon Street   Cannon Street
CANNON STREET
Via Woodside
FIRST CLASS   THIRD CLASS
Fare /9 H   Fare /9 H
NOT TRANSFERABLE

2123
W. & S. C. Jt. Line.

Down		Up
1111111 / 1111111	Bingham Rd. & Woodside	1111111 / 1111111
1111111 / 1111111	Bingham Rd. & Coombe Lane	1111111 / 1111111
1111111 / 1111111	Spencer Rd. & Coombe Lane	1111111 / 1111111
1111111 / 1111111	Spencer Rd. & Selsdon Road	1111111 / 1111111
1½1½1½1½ / 1½1½1½1½	Bingham Rd. & Spencer Road	1½1½1½1½ / 1½1½1½1½
22222222 / 22222222	Bingham Rd. & Selsdon Road	22222222 / 22222222
22222222 / 22222222	Spencer Rd. & Woodside	22222222 / 22222222
2½2½2½2½ / 2½2½2½2½	Woodside & Selsdon Road	2½2½2½2½ / 2½2½2½2½
33333333 / 33333333	Dogs	33333333 / 33333333

SINGLE JOURNEY
(See back)

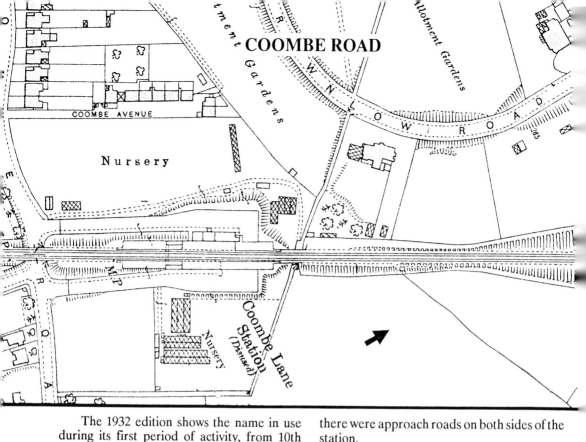

The 1932 edition shows the name in use during its first period of activity, from 10th August 1885 until 1st January 1917. Note that there were approach roads on both sides of the station.

9. The lower signal arm is on a nearer post than the other two in this southward view. Traffic was scant. In the first half of 1889, for example, the numbers of passengers carried on the line were 48 first class, 259 second and 8767 third. There was a substantial loss in every year except one up to 1900. The signal box was seldom used. (Lens of Sutton)

10. A northward view shows Coombe Lane Tunnel (157 yds), beyond which is Park Hill Tunnel (122 yds) and Woodside Tunnel (166 yds); all were closely spaced. The Whitgift Hospital Estate demanded one tunnel, the others being built due to cutting instability. (G.D.Metherell)

11. Agreement was reached soon after opening that the LBSCR and SER would work the trains for a year alternately, commencing on July 1st each year. (From 1899 the latter were run by the South Eastern & Chatham Railway.) Steam railmotors of this type were used for economy. For example, SECR no. 2 was noted in 1910 and LBSCR nos 1 and 2 in 1913. (Lens of Sutton)

12. Despite the line's appalling financial history, the SR was able to obtain public funding in the 1930s for its refurbishment and electrification. Here we witness more money being spent, this time on platform lengthening in May 1956, for 10-coach trains. (Pamlin Prints)

13. Consideration was given to closing the line in 1894, as it was losing over £1000 per annum, but legal problems prevented it. A northward view in the 1960s shows that the station was then still complete but the down canopy did not last until closure. (Pamlin Prints)

The Croydon Tramlink Act was passed in July 1994 for a tramway to join Wimbledon with Beckenham Junction. A branch to New Addington would run parallel to Coombe Road and new track would be laid on the route over which we have just travelled. The BR line from Elmers End to Addiscombe would be closed and the part south of Blackhorse Road abandoned. Other Middleton Press albums (with picture numbers) that give further details are *Clapham Junction to Beckenham Junction* (107), *London Bridge to Addiscombe* (120), *Mitcham Junction Lines* (103) and *Croydon's Tramways* (121).

14. The SR erected one of its Odeon-style masterpieces on the up side. It was pathetic irony, on such a financially disastrous line, that the booking office here was closed in 1981, owing to the conviction of its clerk for fraud. (Pamlin Prints)

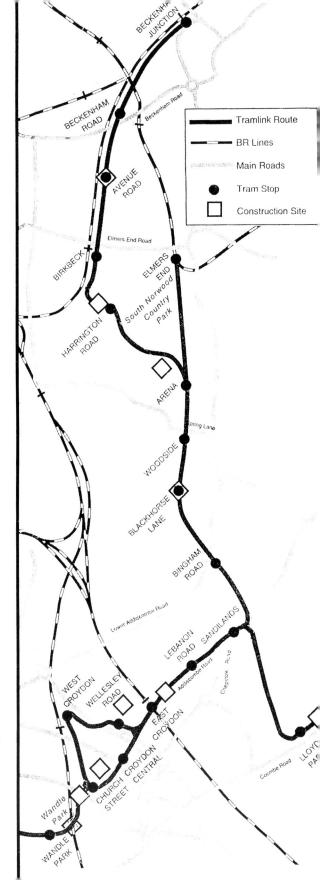

SPENCER ROAD HALT

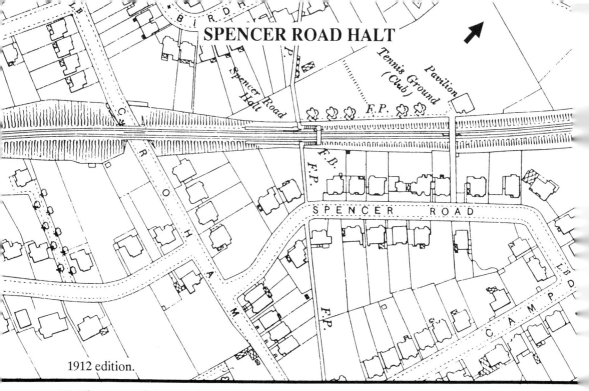

1912 edition.

15. The two 100ft long timber platforms came into use on 1st September 1906 when rail-motors were introduced. This 1922 southward view shows that the footbridge was a short distance from the platforms. The notice states "This gate is for the use of passengers proceeding to and from the platforms. Pedestrians must pass over the railway by means of the footbridge." (H.J.Patterson Rutherford)

16. Class E 4-4-0 no. A175 passes through on 13th September 1931 with a Hastings excursion southbound. The halt had closed temporarily on 15th March 1915 but it never reopened. (H.C.Casserley)

B **7033**

W. & S. C. Jt. Line

Down		Up
11111111 11111111	Bingham Rd. & Woodside	11111111 11111111
11111111 11111111	Bingham Rd. & Coombe L'ne	11111111 11111111
11111111 11111111	Spencer Road & Coombe L'ne	11111111 11111111
11111111 11111111	Spencer Road & Selsdon Rd.	11111111 11111111
1½1½1½1½ 1½1½1½1½	Bingham Rd. & Spencer Rd.	1½1½1½1½ 1½1½1½1½
22222222 22222222	Bingham Rd. & Selsdon Rd.	22222222 22222222
22222222 22222222	Spencer Road & Woodside	222 32 222 22
2½2½2½2½ 2½2½2½2½	Woodside & Selsdon Rd.	2½2½2½2½ 2½2½2½2½
33333333 33333333	Dogs	33333333 33333333

SINGLE JOURNEY.
(S Back.)

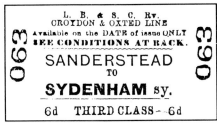

L. B. & S. C. Ry.
CROYDON & OXTED LINE
Available on the DATE of issue ONLY
SEE CONDITIONS AT BACK.

SANDERSTEAD
TO
SYDENHAM sy.

6d   THIRD CLASS — 6d

063   063

2478

W. & S. C. Jt. Line.

Bingham Rd. Halt to Woodside	11111 11111
Bingham Rd. Halt to Coombe Lane	11111111 11111111
Spencer Rd. Halt to Coombe Lane	11111111 11111111
Spencer Rd. Halt to Selsdon Road	11111111 11111111
Bingham Rd. Halt to Spencer Rd Halt	1½1½1½1½ 1½1½1½1½
Spencer Rd. Halt to Bingham Rd. Halt	1½1½1½1½ 1½1½1½1½
Bingham Rd. Halt to Selsdon Road	22222222 22222222
Spencer Rd. Halt to Woodside	22222222 22222222
Dogs	33333333 33333333

SINGLE JOURNEY.

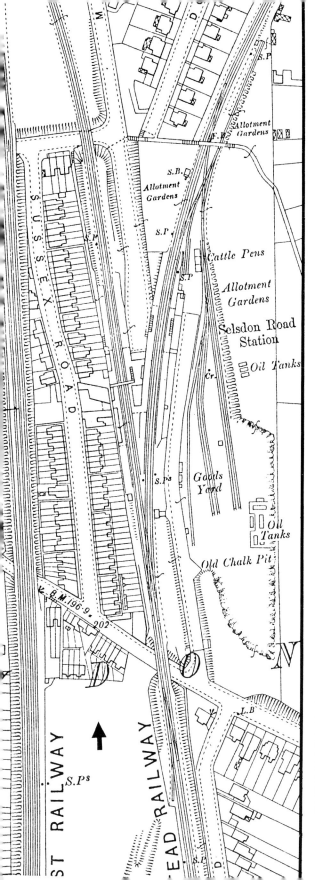

SELSDON

17. An LBSCR coach is in the dock road as we look north towards Woodside and North Box. Note that both platforms are signalled for starting up trains. (G.D.Metherell)

18. Junction Box is in view as we look south and notice that the sign board is of a different style (LBSCR) from the previous one seen (SECR). The differing signals originated from the same companies. The ringed arms are for calling on during shunting movements. (G.D.Metherell)

The 1913 edition has the line from Woodside top right and that to East Grinstead lower right. On the left are the quadruple tracks of the London - Brighton main line. Selsdon Road itself crosses the map diagonally and gave its name to the station when it opened (probably) on 10th August 1885. It first appeared in Bradshaw's September 1885 timetable. The crane (marked Cr.) could lift 10 tons.

19. Here is a typical LBSCR suburban train of the type used before the introduction of railmotors. No. 70 *Poplar* was one of the popular "Terrier" class designed for London local services and is now on the Kent & East Sussex Railway. North Box was abolished on 22nd September 1935. The guard has a cash bag for fares from the halts for which he issued bell-punch tickets. (J.B.Gent Coll.)

20. The D1 class 0-4-2Ts took over much of the "Terrier" work in the suburbs before electrification. No. 2253 is entering the down main platform as it accelerates the 6.36pm East Croydon to Tunbridge Wells West train on 10th May 1949. This is the rear portion of the 6.10pm from Victoria. The front part ran non-stop from East Croydon to Oxted and continued to Uckfield where it arrived at 7.38. (G.Bloxham/D.Cullum Coll.)

21. The 10.37am special from London Bridge to Maidstone West is running in from the Woodside direction on 9th September 1950. Class U no. 31639 would later use the Crowhurst Spur to convey its train of hop pickers to Kent. (J.J.Smith)

22. Seen from the footbridge in the previous picture is Q class no. 30544. It is shunting the yard while working the 6.27pm Oxted to Norwood Junction freight on 21st May 1952. The cattle dock is also in the view. (S.C.Nash)

23.   A northward panorama from the footbridge in May 1955 includes signalling in
transition and a train in South Croydon station.
There was a better train service to London
from this station and most local residents used
it in preference to Selsdon which lost its suffix
"Road" on 30th September 1935. (D.Cullum)

24. Turning round, the photographer recorded the junction and the 1935 conductor rails, together with a private siding. This was used by Blackwells & National Roofing in 1934. The lines in the foreground received conductor rails in 1981 to allow some down London trains that terminated at East Croydon to do so at Sanderstead during track alterations. (D.Cullum)

25. The Woodside line platforms (right) were linked by a subway. The station closed entirely on 1st January 1917 but the main line platforms were reopened on 1st March 1919 and they finally closed on 14th June 1959. Prior to that date, trains called on weekday mornings only at 8.17, 8.26 and 8.52 up, the only down train being the 8.30 to Tunbridge Wells West. (Lens of Sutton)

26. This southward view shows both roadways to the station and that the up starting signal for the down line had been moved away from the platform - compare with picture no. 22. The up starter was repositioned close to the foot-bridge from which this picture was taken. A few electric trains terminated here. The goods yard was in use for general traffic from 1884 until 17th October 1968. (J.B.Gent Coll.)

27. Largely abandoned by passengers, the station assumed the air of a derelict rural outpost although firmly in the suburbs. This is the approach from the north, when the only option to London after 8.52am was a slow train on the Mid-Kent, with a change at Elmers End. (J.B.Gent Coll.)

28. DEMU no. 1313 leads as the six-coach 09.45 from Hurst Green rushes past the remaining signal box on 18th July 1969. It had 22 levers when opened and was in use until 1st April 1984. Units 1301-19 were built for Oxted services and each had 24 first-class and 160 second-class seats. (J.Scrace)

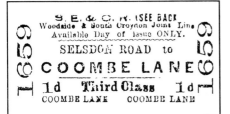

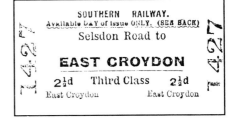

29. All the buildings were eventually demolished and a ticket hut was erected. This is visible to the right of the 2EPB working the 16.00 from Elmers End on 21st May 1971. The down side canopy was blown down on 12th November 1977 and the up one was dismantled later that month. The track was still in situ in 1995. (D.Gould)

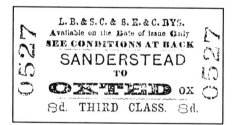

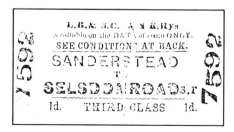

30. The Anglo-American Oil Company established an oil depot in the yard in 1894 and the sidings remained in use until March 1993 when the effects of the government's railway policy terminated a century of good work. No. 47369 leaves the sidings on 18th March 1993. The run-round loop extended as far as the Fairway Path footbridge seen in picture no 16. (A.Dasi-Sutton)

SANDERSTEAD

31. The station opened with the line on 10th March 1884 and this northward view is dated May of that year. Footbridge glazing followed later. The population at this time was a little over 300 and increased to only 534 by 1901. The station is one mile from, and 300 ft below, the village centre. (J.B.Gent Coll.)

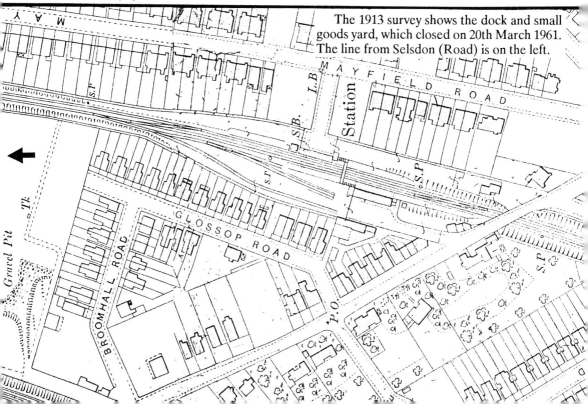

The 1913 survey shows the dock and small goods yard, which closed on 20th March 1961. The line from Selsdon (Road) is on the left.

32. Included in this postcard view is an extensive bookstall, part of the goods yard and the junction distant signals for Selsdon Road, below the up starting signal. (Lens of Sutton)

33. The 4.50pm Victoria to Brighton (via Uckfield) is leaving Sanderstead on 26th June 1954 behind no. 34039 *Boscastle*. As this was a Saturday, through carriages to Tunbridge Wells were not conveyed. On the right is the final length of conductor rail, used by terminating trains. (S.C.Nash)

34. A little further south, but with the same building in the background, we witness the passing of no. 34027 *Taw Valley*, a rebuilt version of the "West Country" class seen in the previous picture. It is working the 4.40pm London Bridge to Brighton (via Uckfield) on 26th April 1963 and is now to be found on the Severn Valley Railway. (J.Scrace)

35. Still in green livery, unit no. 1318 forms part of the 15.55 Victoria to Uckfield on 11th June 1969. The up platform had been extended across the entrance to the goods yard to accommodate nine coaches. The signal box closed on 2nd November 1985 and was demolished in August 1987. (J.Scrace)

36. The timber clad buildings beloved by both the LBSCR and the SER were cheap but required considerable maintenance, which was a small problem with low cost labour of Victorian times. This is one of the station's unattractive phases between repaints. (C.Hall)

37. No. 33038 passes with the 17.34 London Bridge to East Grinstead on 25th July 1980. There were four locomotive hauled trains each way in 1973 but, by the time of their demise on 13th May 1983, there were only two. (J.S.Petley)

38. No. 5764 waits to work the 17.57 back to Elmers End on 11th April 1983, having used the crossover in the background. At that time fewer than 150 people used the trains on that route each day. The crossover was still in use in 1995; the 06.42 up train started here. (A.Dasi-Sutton)

L. B. & S. C. Ry.
CROYDON & OXTED LINE.
Available on the Date of Issue Only.
This Ticket is issued subject to the Regulations
& Conditions stated in the Company's Time
Tables & Bills.
SANDERSTEAD
TO
EAST CROYDON [MAIN]
2d. THIRD CLASS 2d.
3486   3486

L. B. & S. C. RY.
CROYDON & OXTED LINE.
Available on the **DATE** of issue **ONLY.**
This Ticket is issued subject to the Regulations
& Conditions stated in the Company's Time
Tables & Bills.
SANDERSTEAD
TO
LONDON
1s.0d. THIRD CLASS. 1s.0d.
7897   7897

39. The wooden building was destroyed by fire in June 1986. An up train is drawing in on 15th August 1993 as we admire the imaginative style of its replacement. (M.J.Stretton)

40. The signal box was demolished in 1987 but the original footbridge was retained during the rebuilding. The clean lines of the new building complement the modernised electrified route. (J.Scrace)

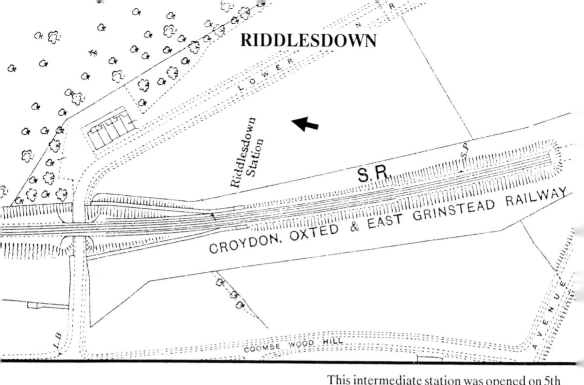

RIDDLESDOWN

This intermediate station was opened on 5th June 1927 to encourage housing development in this unspoilt part of Surrey. The 1934 edition reveals that there were still many vacant plots.

41. A southward view in the 1950s shows gas lights and that some house building had taken place in the vicinity of the station. (Pamlin Prints)

42. BR class 4 2-6-4T no. 80012 is bound for Victoria on 2nd April 1960. The condition of locomotives and coaches left a lot to be desired at that time but electric platform lighting had arrived. (T.Wright)

43. Yet more new lighting was evident, together with the 1957 building, when DEMU no. 1120 was photographed on 23rd November 1985. This was one of the 3H type built for use on the Hampshire secondary routes. (T.Wright)

44. Emerging from the southern portal of the 836yd long Riddlesdown Tunnel on 16th April 1960 is class 4 no. 80017. Riddlesdown Tunnel Intermediate Box was situated 180 yds south of the tunnel and was in use until 20th June 1948. (T.Wright)

45. The 3.52pm Victoria to Brighton was hauled by diesel-electric no. 10800 on 25th April 1953. It was built by the North British Locomotive Company in 1950. The train carried an Eastbourne portion which was detached at Eridge. (N.W.Sprinks)

46. Class H1 4-4-2 no. 39 runs across Riddlesdown Viaduct with a Brighton to Victoria via East Grinstead train in about 1909. All three of the CO&EGR viaducts were of this complex rivetted lattice structure. (W.S.Gray/A.C.Ingram Coll.)

47. A cement works was in production under the viaduct until 1969 but there was no rail connection to it. A 2-6-4T is southbound on 14th October 1956. (T.Wright)

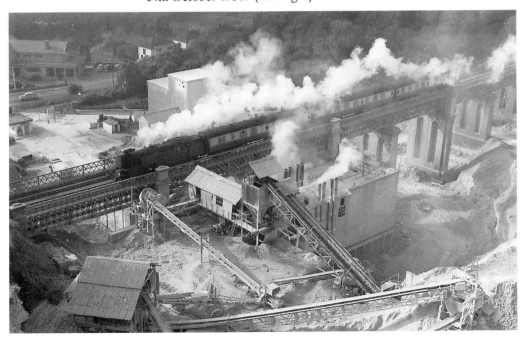

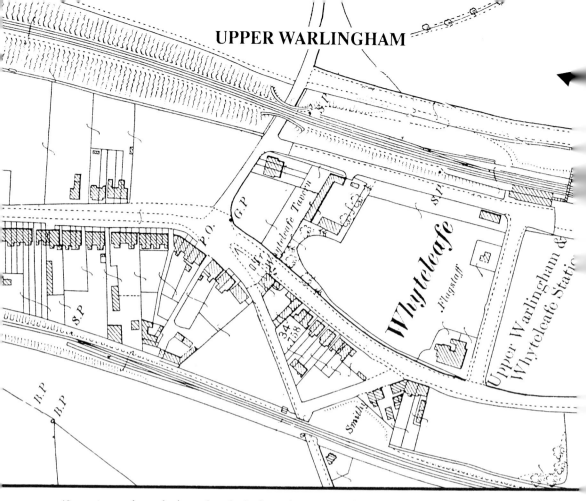

48. A southward view shortly before the opening includes a single point rod for the down siding. A crossover was added later, necessitating more rods. Warlingham grew from 1100 in 1881 to 2500 in 1901 in response to the arrival of the railway. (Lens of Sutton)

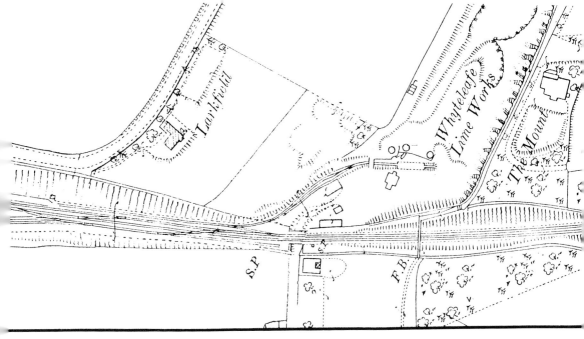

The 1894 survey carries the full name of the station, the suffix having been added on 1st January 1894. It was dropped in 1900. Lower left (and on the valley floor) is a siding on the Caterham branch at the site of the 1900 Whyteleafe station - see our *Caterham & Tattenham Corner* album for details.

49. Class B4 4-4-0 no. 2048 arrives from London Bridge with a Birdcage set, the top of the goods crane appearing by its dome. The SR eventually abolished most lower quadrant signals of this type, along with wooden posts. (D.Cullum Coll.)

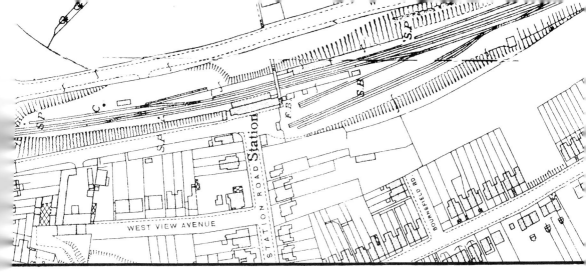

50. The end-loading dock is visible as class E5 0-6-2T no. 32574 waits with the 5.14pm Tunbridge Wells West to East Croydon service on 16th June 1950. Its journey ended at 6.45pm, having called at all but three stations. The engine returned with the 7.24pm East Croydon to Groombridge train. (S.C.Nash)

The 1934 edition reveals the extent of building development in the area and of coal siding expansion. The dock siding near the signal box was the first and was laid in 1892. The crane (marked C.) was listed as having 4 tons 12 cwt capacity).

51. The line to Nichols' limeworks had been to the right of the picture. The train is the 4.50pm Victoria to Brighton via Uckfield on 16th July 1951 and the locomotive is no. 31909 of class U1. The stationmaster's house of 1893 is in the distance. (S.C.Nash)

52. The 3.28pm Haywards Heath to London Bridge was regularly hauled by a K class 2-6-0 for many years, although they were mainly used for freight work. No. 32346 was recorded near the coal pens on 25th April 1953. (N.W.Sprinks)

53. The timber roadway for coal carts had gone when class U1 no. 31907 was photographed with the 6.5pm Oxted - Norwood Junction freight on 6th June 1962. Steam was nearing terminal decline in the area and loose coupled wagons were to be eliminated as soon as possible. (S.C.Nash)

54. The goods yard closed on 4th May 1964 and most of the track had gone when the signal box was pictured in 1969. That closed on 2nd November 1985. (J.Scrace)

S. E. R.
CROYDON & OXTED JOINT LINE
UPPER WARLINGHAM TO
CANNON STREET
Via East Croydon
1/3   Third   1/3
Children over 3 and under 12 years
half fares under 3 years free

3759   3759

2nd · SINGLE   SINGLE · 2nd
Upper Warlingham to
Upper Warlingham   Upper Warlingham
Woldingham   Woldingham
WOLDINGHAM
(S)   0/3   Fare   0/3   (S)
For conditions see over   For conditions see over

0504   0504

55. As a preliminary publicity event, a Gala Weekend was held on 26-27th September 1987, a week before the full electric timetable was introduced. Temporary 15ins gauge track was laid in the car park for the Romney Hythe & Dymchurch Railway's *The Bug*, which is of German origin. (A.Dasi-Sutton)

56. The outline of the original building was recognisable in 1992 despite its modern coating. Passengers were expected to fumble for tickets from the machine in the rain although the platforms still had canopies. (J.Scrace)

57. Woldingham Viaduct stands as a monument to the Surrey & Sussex Junction Railway, having been built by that company in about 1865. Viaduct technology had advanced by the time the line was completed nearly 20 years later. The line climbs at 1 in 100 for half a mile from here to the station. (E.Jackson Coll.)

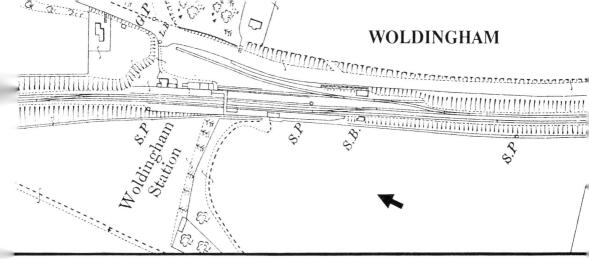

S.P.

Woldingham
Station

S.P.

S.B.

S.P.

The 1912 issue shows the rural location of the station, a situation which still applies today. It opened on 1st July 1885. South of the station, the route passes through the 1 mile 506yd long Oxted Tunnel which is on a 1 in 132 falling gradient for down trains.

58. The rustic charm of the station approach was conveyed well by this Edwardian postcard. The main siding terminates behind the sign board. The station was named "Marden Park" until 1st January 1894. (Lens of Sutton)

59. A February 1953 photograph includes the signal box that closed on 2nd November 1985. The station receives more snow than most in the area as it is at 450 ft above sea level. The summit of the line is half a mile to the south. (D.Cullum)

L. B. & S. C. Ry.
Available on the DATE of issue ONLY
This Ticket is issued subject to the Regulations
& Conditions stated in the Company's Time
Tables & Bills
1083   WOLDINGHAM   1083
TO
E'ST GRINSTEAD [L.L.] e.g.
1s.0½d. Third Class. 1s.0½d.

L. B. & S. C.   S. E. Rwy.
Croydon & Oxted Joint Line
0960   MARDEN PARK   0960
TO
E. CROYDON e.c.
THIRD CLASS.   7d.
[See Back

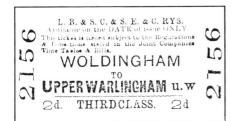

60. Brighton-built BR class 4 no. 80086 has a great excess of steam as it pauses on its 1 in 100 climb with the 5.40pm London Bridge to East Grinstead on 23rd June 1954. The seven coaches would have been packed with City workers for the first part of the journey. Only the front three coaches continued beyond East Grinstead, as the 7.6pm to Lewes. (R.C.Riley)

61. The village grew slowly from 132 in 1871 to 220 in 1901. This is the east elevation in 1955. The station cost £3750 of which £500 was provided by a local landowner. (R.C.J.Day)

63. A Victoria to East Grinstead service arrives on 30th March 1994, the station then being remarkably little changed since the time when hordes of excursionists arrived for a day in the nearby park. Crossovers were added in 1887 for this traffic. (M.Turvey)

62. The goods yard closed on 4th May 1959 but the dock siding was retained by the engineers for many years. The Hampshire DEMUs had their first class compartments at one end, whereas the Oxted units had theirs in the middle of the centre coach. (C.Hall)

64.   One mile north of the station the line passed under a SSJR brick built bridge (left) which carried a lane to Oxted Lime Works, for which a private siding was provided in 1886. A class D3 0-4-4T hauls a down train, which is viewed from Oxted Lime Sidings signal box in about 1902. Near the engine shed is one of the two Manning Wardle saddle tanks known to have worked the line. A new vertical boilered Sentinel was purchased in 1927 and sold to Hall & Co. at Coulsdon in 1948, although the sidings do not seem to have been used after 1939. (National Railway Museum)

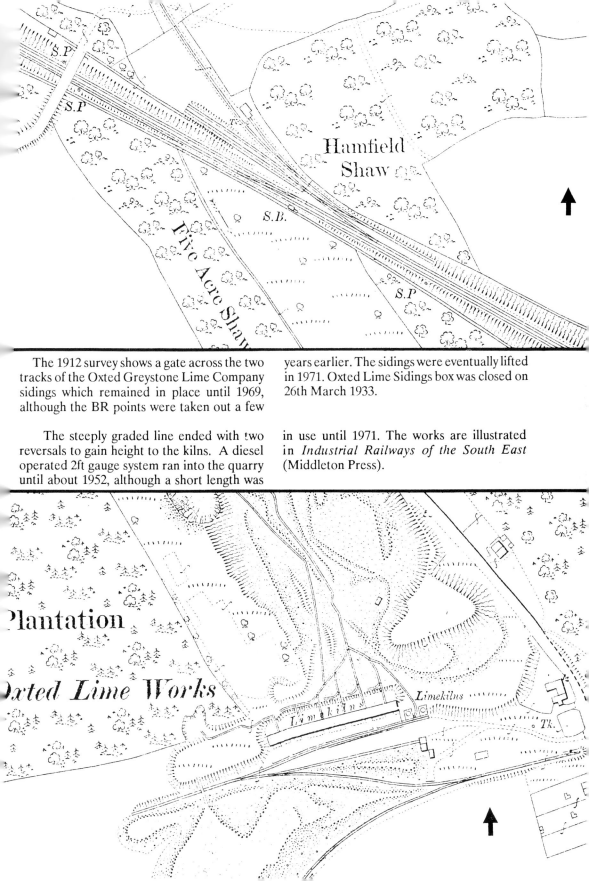

S.P

S.P

Hamfield
Shaw

Five Acre Shaw

S.B.

S.P

The 1912 survey shows a gate across the two tracks of the Oxted Greystone Lime Company sidings which remained in place until 1969, although the BR points were taken out a few years earlier. The sidings were eventually lifted in 1971. Oxted Lime Sidings box was closed on 26th March 1933.

The steeply graded line ended with two reversals to gain height to the kilns. A diesel operated 2ft gauge system ran into the quarry until about 1952, although a short length was in use until 1971. The works are illustrated in *Industrial Railways of the South East* (Middleton Press).

Plantation

Oxted Lime Works

Limekilns

Limekilns

Tk.

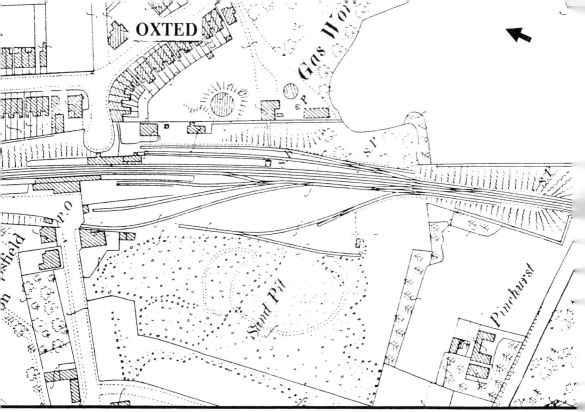

OXTED

The 1896 survey marks a coal shute into the premises of the Oxted & Limpsfield Gas Company , which was established in 1885. Its sidings were opened in 1892. By 1920 the works was consuming 1734 tons of coal per annum but was absorbed by its Croydon neighbour soon after. The warehouse (near the road) was added in 1896.

65. The station opened with the line and served the two communities shown on the running-in board, although Limpsfield is nearly one mile to the east. (Lens of Sutton)

66. In the background of this postcard view are the North Downs, through which the line passes in Oxted Tunnel. The 1 in 100 descent eases to 1 in 300 through the station. (Lens of Sutton)

The 1933 edition shows building and siding development, together with the location of the crane which was of 6-ton capacity.

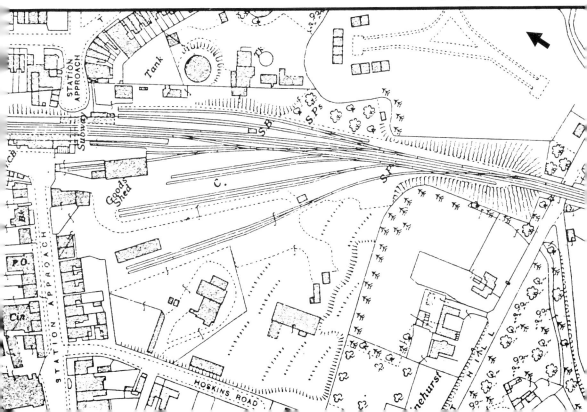

67. A southward panorama on 16th June 1923 includes the gasworks siding and much of the goods yard, which was in use until 6th January 1969. In 1914 the station handled 92 trains each weekday, 67 of these being operated by the LBSCR. (Late E. Wallis)

L. B. & S. C. RY.
Available on the DATE of issue ONLY.
This ticket is issued subject to the Regulations
& Conditions stated in the Company's Time
Tables & Bills

OXTED
TO
HEATHFIELD
THIRD CLASS.
3/9½ Revised Fare. 3/9½

4675

L. B. & S. C. Ry.
Available on the DATE of issue ONLY.
SEE CONDITIONS ON BACK.
MOTOR CAR SERVICE.
OXTED STATION TO
HURST GREEN HALT
1d. THIRD CLASS. 1d.

5205

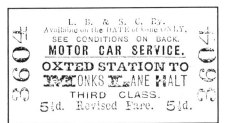

L. B. & S. C. Ry.
Available on the DATE of issue ONLY.
SEE CONDITIONS ON BACK.
MOTOR CAR SERVICE.
OXTED STATION TO
MONKS LANE HALT
THIRD CLASS.
5½d. Revised Fare. 5½d.

6604

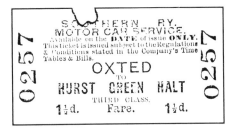

SOUTHERN RY.
MOTOR CAR SERVICE.
Available on the DATE of issue ONLY.
This ticket is issued subject to the Regulations
& Conditions stated in the Company's Time
Tables & Bills

OXTED
TO
HURST GREEN HALT
THIRD CLASS.
1½d. Fare. 1½d.

0257

68. The signal box was erected in 1896 and was photographed in 1923, along with a gas holder. One of these was still standing in 1995. The box was in use until 11th July 1987, when it was replaced by a panel box. (Late E.Wallis)

69. A barrow crossing was provided at the north end of the station. This was recorded in August 1948 while a C2X obstructed it and a down train braked on the steep gradient. (D.Clayton)

70. Pictured on 13th September 1948 are class Q no. 540 in the goods yard, class I3 no. 2075 on the 3.55pm Oxted to Brighton via Sheffield Park and class D1 no. 2253 in the bay, which was added in 1889. The water tank is also visible. (H.C.Casserley Coll.)

71. Class U1 no. 31910 waits with a down train from Victoria on 1st August 1955, while a push-pull service stands in the bay. The former trains arrived at 57 minutes past each hour and continued to Tunbridge Wells West via East Grinstead, while the latter departed at 04 and ran direct (via Edenbridge Town) to the same destination, arriving 19 minutes earlier. (J.H.Aston)

72. "Schools" class no. 30936 *Cranleigh* arrives with the 4.48pm from Victoria on 19th July 1961, four coaches being for Brighton and three for Tunbridge Wells West. These were detached at Ashurst. The 4.38pm push-pull from Tonbridge has just arrived in the up platform at 5.37. The platforms were gas lit from 1892 until about 1969. (R.S.Greenwood)

73. Seen on 13th September 1963 is a unique formation of five 4SUB trailer coaches assembled between two 2BIL driving coaches hauled by D6529. This train was used in the peak hours and, being air braked and electrically heated, was compatible with diesel locomotives. No. D6550 is in the yard. (S.C.Nash)

74. As elsewhere, the timber clad building was rendered and finished with pebble-dash to prolong its life (in theory). This is the up side, access to the subway being on the right. (C.Hall)

75. The Venice Simplon Orient Express Pullmans were used on a special train to Hever on 2nd October 1984, hauled by no. 33042. Several sidings were used by the engineers or for berthing DEMUs. (J.Scrace)

76. Nos. 207014 and 207019 form the East Grinstead portion of the 12.36 from Victoria on 27th December 1986. A 2EPB has been shunted into the dock and chocked to serve as a temporary waiting room, as rebuilding of the station had just commenced. (A.Dasi-Sutton)

77. Lighting of the new booking hall in daytime was achieved by a dormer window and a perfect anti-graffiti surface was applied to the subway - irregular coloured tile fragments. It gives a pleasing effect that could be copied nationally to great benefit. (J.Scrace)

78. 4VEP no. 3503 passes the sole electrified berthing siding as it works the 11.38 East Grinstead to Victoria on 30th March 1994, while DEMU no. 205005 waits in the bay to leave for Uckfield at 12.04. The new building (centre) houses the signalling panel that controls both branches. It was at this panel that a signalman watched helplessly as two DEMUs ran towards each other on 15th October 1994, before colliding head on near Cowden. (M.Turvey)

79. On the left is the 1987 up side building; the down side canopy did not appear until the early part of 1990. Type 3H no. 205029 forms the 12.47 East Croydon to Uckfield service on 12th July 1994. This and a corresponding mid-day up train ran from 13th May 1991 until 14th October 1994. After electrification, there were only four up and down through trains between Uckfield and London, weekdays only. (J.Scrace)

SOUTH OF OXTED

80. The station is in the background as class I1X no. 2002 runs on to Limpsfield Viaduct with the 3.35pm Oxted to Brighton on 30th June 1951, shortly before the locomotive's withdrawal. An SECR Birdcage set is in tow. (G.F.Bloxham)

81. An H class 0-4-4T propels two Maunsell coaches, forming an Oxted to Tunbridge Wells West train, over Limpsfield Viaduct on 13th April 1963. The houses came long after the viaduct, despite the noise. (S.J.Greenwood)

82. Immediately after crossing the viaduct, trains plunge into the 565 yd long Limpsfield Tunnel. Class I2 4-4-2T no. 12 is emerging from it in 1923, with a Tunbridge Wells West to London Bridge train. (Lens of Sutton)

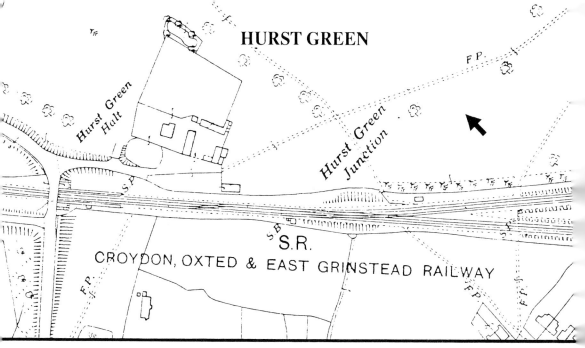

HURST GREEN

S.R.
CROYDON, OXTED & EAST GRINSTEAD RAILWAY

The junction came into use on 2nd January 1888 when the line to Edenbridge (Town) opened. The halt followed on 1st June 1907 when motor trains were introduced on that route. This is the 1933 edition.

83. The post on the left carried a stay wire to the junction signals, which had to be elevated so that they could be seen above the road bridge. Class D3 no. 2380 is bound for Brighton via Sheffield Park, sometime in the 1930s. (J.R.W.Kirkby coll.)

84. The short platforms were recorded in January 1953 at which time 15 East Grinstead and 14 Tunbridge Wells trains called on weekdays. On Sundays there were seven down trains. (D.Cullum)

85. The platforms were rebuilt to a much greater length north of the road bridge and opened on 12th June 1961, the word "Halt" then being dropped. BR class 4 no. 80151 arrives with the 3.8pm Victoria - Tunbridge Wells West via East Grinstead on 22nd July 1961, when the concrete slabs were still pure white. (R.S.Greenwood)

> **Oxted and Hurst Green both appear in *Branch Lines to East Grinstead* and *Branch Lines to Tunbridge Wells*, other photographs and maps being contained therein.**

86. The original plan was for trains to divide and join up here and so ample staff accommodation was provided for train crews and shunters. The 12.04 Oxted to Uckfield calls on 12th July 1994, having followed closely on the heels of the East Grinstead electric. (J.Scrace)

HURST GREEN JUNCTION

87. LBSCR class E5 0-6-2T no. 572 *Farncombe* is viewed from the signal box as it steams north with seven coaches. This is a special train, probably from Lingfield in connection with the races. (Lens of Sutton)

88. The typical LBSCR-pattern signal box with top lights was photographed on 31st January 1953. It remained in use until 11th July 1987 and was demolished two months later. (D.Cullum)

89.   Class Q1 no. 33032 passes over new flat bottom rails on 31st August 1957, the old bullhead ones lying alongside. It is heading the 2.35pm London Bridge to Maidstone West special and will take the next turning left, at Crowhurst Junction. (J.J.Smith)

CROWHURST JUNCTION

90.   Having worked empty from London Bridge at 08.52 on 21st January 1970, 3D units nos. 1316 and 1310 reverse over the crossover in front of the signal box to form the 09.45 Hurst Green to Victoria, the only train to start here at that period. The Uckfield line curves left behind the rear coach. It was cut short at that town on 23rd February 1969. (D.Gould)

91.   A down hop pickers special leaves the East Grinstead route in the late summer of 1956. Class D1 4-4-0 no. 31741 is hauling entirely ex-SECR stock. Regular services over this curve officially ceased on 10th June 1955 but, owing to the ASLEF strike, the last scheduled train was on 27th May of that year, although a railtour used the spur on 3rd January 1965. (N.W.Sprinks)

92. These are the signals to be found in the distance in the previous picture. This was the limit of joint ownership, SER trains bearing left here on to that company's original main line from Redhill to Tonbridge, now an international freight route. The U1 class 4-6-0 is no. 31897 and it is working the 4.48pm Lingfield to Victoria on 1st July 1961. Crowhurst Junction North Box (right) and South Box both closed on 25th October 1965. (J.J.Smith)

93. Slightly over one mile south of Crowhurst Junction was Lingfield Intermediate Box. In addition to being a block post, it controlled the sidings to the Crowhurst Brick & Tile Works. Note that there were gates across both sidings. On 10th August 1958, the box was replaced by a ground frame which was electrically released from Limpsfield station box. Seen in 1953, the sidings were usable until about 1970. (D.Cullum)

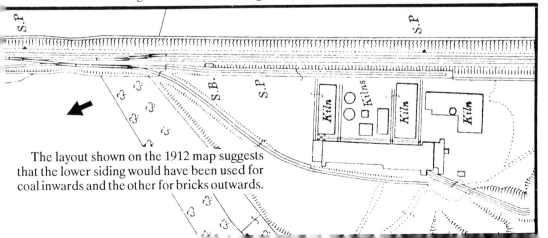

The layout shown on the 1912 map suggests that the lower siding would have been used for coal inwards and the other for bricks outwards.

LINGFIELD

94. Two footbridges were available for many years, to enable the crowds to leave the down platform quickly and walk to the racecourse. Some empty trains were berthed in East Grinstead goods yard during the races. (Lens of Sutton)

The 1912 survey features the down loop and sidings used on race days. These were added in 1894, the racecourse having opened in 1890. The station opened with the line.

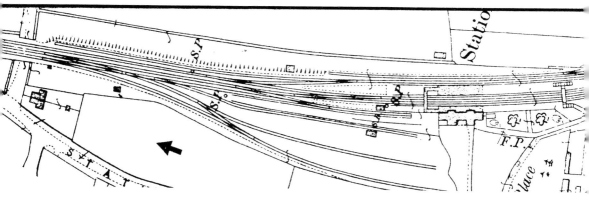

95. A 1951 view includes two of the berthing sidings in the foreground. Note that both footbridges were covered at that time. Loco-motives were turned by running up the goods spur at East Grinstead and returning via the St. Margarets curve. (Pamlin Prints)

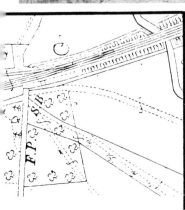

96. Seen at the south end of the station in 1961 is the ground frame cabin. Also evident is part of the long covered walkway to the race course. The roof and the cabin have both long gone and the near footbridge has been moved to Sheffield Park on the Bluebell Railway. (D.Cullum)

97.   Between the wars there were often six extra trains on race days. The number declined but here is an impressive one returning to Victoria behind BR class 4 no. 75074 on 7th June 1963, complete with a Pullman Car in the formation. There were only two specials that year. The goods headshunt is in the foreground. (S.C.Nash)

98.   Recorded on the same day is a train of banana vans from Avonmouth Docks standing at the ripening sheds of Geest Industries. This traffic ceased in October 1971, general goods traffic having stopped on 5th August 1968. The signal box closed on 11th July 1987 having, in its latter years, only been used in the peak hours. (J.Scrace)

99.　Narrow-bodied Hastings line DEMUs formed a railtour named "Oxted Line Diesel Sunset" on 5th September 1987, although some were to continue running in their twilight years. The final steam special had been hauled by "West Country" no. 34102 *Lapford* on the "Surrey Downsman" on 5th March 1967. (A.Dasi-Sutton)

100.　The bunting was out on 30th September 1987 to celebrate the completion of the long-overdue electrification and doubling of the train service. Race crowds have for many years been accommodated by simply lengthening timetabled trains. (J.Scrace)

DORMANS

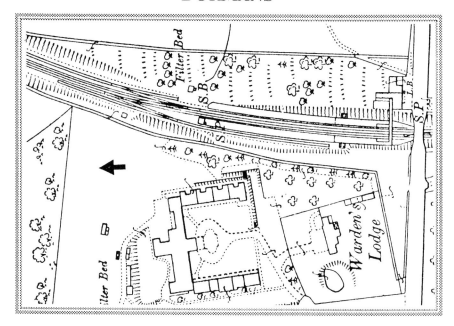

The 1912 map indicates the position of the up siding which was used for coal supplies to the nearby building, no public goods facilities being provided here. There is a down refuge siding, a crossover and a signal box.

101. Like Lingfield, the station opened with the line but its buildings were away from the platforms on higher ground. Ballast over the sleepers was liable to conceal rotten ones; the practice was discontinued a few years after the line came into use. (Lens of Sutton)

102. The station is situated on a country lane in a sparsely populated district. The down starting signal is included in this Edwardian view. Apart from its absence, little had changed in 1995. (Lens of Sutton)

103. Toilets for gentlemen only and canopies were once provided on both platforms, which are on a gradient of 1 in 210, an easing of the 1 in 70 up all the way from Lingfield. This is a 1951 southward view. (Pamlin Prints)

104. Owing to the cost of maintenance at this lightly used station, the roof was removed from the steps on the down side and both canopies were dismantled. At least the train frequency doubled in 1987. (C.Hall)

105. Nearly one mile south of the station, the line passes over Cooks Pond Viaduct, seen soon after completion when the pond was still drained. Dorman Park had a private siding north of the viaduct. (Lens of Sutton)

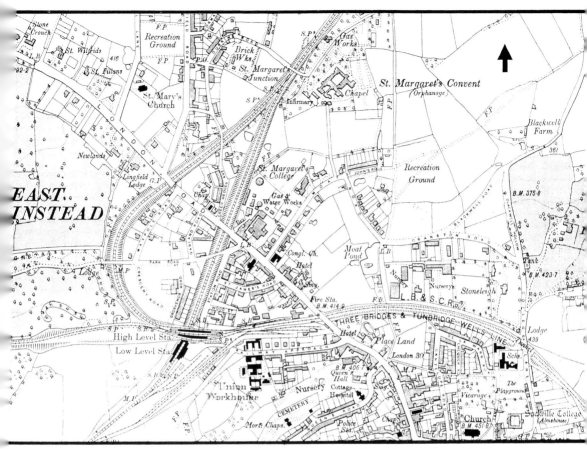

106. An ideal site for those who enjoy fishing and train observation, this tranquil scene was recorded in 1954 and was unchanged forty years later. The pond is fed by a small stream which flows from it, under the railway south of Lingfield and into the River Eden near Edenbridge. (R.C.Riley)

Approaching East Grinstead, the route divided at St. Margarets Junction (top) to give access to Low Level or High Level stations, shown on the 1911 map at 6" to 1 mile. Our line from Dormans is at the top and the one to Lewes is at the bottom. The other is annotated. Two gasworks are shown; the larger consumed 7403 tons of coal in 1936.

107. The 5.9pm Victoria to East Grinstead is signalled for the Low Level on 19th August 1950. It was due in at 6.21pm. Class H2 no. 32422 and its Maunsell set of coaches would work forward to Lewes at 7.7pm. (J.J.Smith)

108. A 1961 photograph shows the Hackenden Lane bridge and the lines to the High Level on the right. This station closed on 1st January 1967; the signal box closed on the next day. The junction was named after the nearby St. Margaret's Convent, which opened in 1870. (D.Cullum)

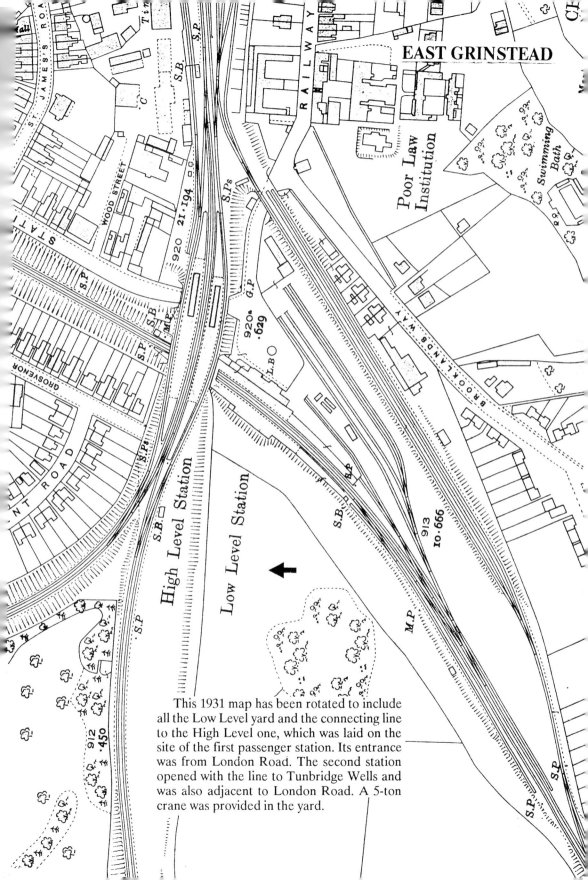

EAST GRINSTEAD

St. JAMES'S ROAD

S.B.

WOOD STREET

STATION

GROSVENOR ROAD

S.P.

S.B.

M.P.

S.Ps

S.B.

S.P.

912 .450

High Level Station

Low Level Station

920 21.194

S.Ps

G.P.

920 .629

L.B.

RAILWAY

Poor Law Institution

Swimming Bath

BROOKLANDS WAY

S.B.

M.P.

913 10.666

S.P.

S.P.

This 1931 map has been rotated to include all the Low Level yard and the connecting line to the High Level one, which was laid on the site of the first passenger station. Its entrance was from London Road. The second station opened with the line to Tunbridge Wells and was also adjacent to London Road. A 5-ton crane was provided in the yard.

109. The 12.3pm Victoria to Brighton approaches the Low Level platforms on 3rd March 1934 having passed under London Road and Park Road bridges. Class D no. 1738 would continue via Sheffield Park to Brighton, where it was due at 2.49pm. (H.C.Casserley)

110. An eastward view from the High Level in the 1930s includes East Box and a London Bridge train arriving from Tunbridge Wells West. On the left is the private siding into Stenning's timber yard. (J.R.W.Kirkby)

111. We look north from the High Level station under which Station Road passes as do the Low Level platforms. All these platforms came into use on 1st August 1882 when the line to Lewes opened. (Lens of Sutton)

112. Turning to the left we catch sight of West Box, with the 1855 Three Bridges lines nearby, and the 1884 Oxted route curving to the right, past the 1922 water tower, whch had been transferred from Streatham Hill. (Lens of Sutton)

113. The 7.5am pick-up goods from Norwood Junction has just passed through the down platform on 9th June 1954, hauled by class C2X no. 32547. South Box is behind the rear brake van. (R.C.Riley)

114. Class 4 2-6-4T no. 42105 is running south with empty stock prior to propelling it back up the spur (right) to the High Level yard on 13th March 1958. The scheme to create the Bluebell Railway further down the line to Lewes was already then in gestation. (R.C.Riley)

115. Loaded coal wagons are in evidence in the lower yard on 16th March 1958, the day that the line southwards closed. Freight facilities were withdrawn at East Grinstead on 10th April 1967. The Southdown PSU/13 Tiger is destined for Brighton via Horsted Keynes. (J.Scrace)

117. No. 601 was a unique 6TC set formed of four ex-6PUL trailers between two 4COR motor cars (with plain bogies). Photographed on 11th June 1966 in a siding adjacent to the Forest Row line, the special connections for experimental push-pull working on the route are apparent. Set 900 (seen in picture no.73) had only centre buffers between the coaches and could not be approved for propelling, whereas these coaches had side buffers. (D.Gould)

116. The Bluebell Railway acquired the track between Sheffield Park and Horsted Keynes, the single line north thereof being lifted in 1964-65. To facilitate this, the demolition contractors hired from the Bluebell their ex-North London Railway 0-6-0T. It is in the Low Level yard on 20th March 1965, having nearly completed its sad task. It later returned by road to its base. (S.C.Nash)

118. The fine Victorian building was demolished in 1971 and replaced by this CLASP structure, attributed to a Consortium of Local Authorities Special Project. The right footbridge in this 1984 photograph is in the position of the High Level station and carries a public footpath. (J.Scrace)

119. The former South Box was recorded on Christmas Day 1980; it remained in use until 17th July 1987. It was latterly provided with a very convenient convenience, although facilities were available halfway along the opposite platform. (D.Gould)

120. The other footbridge in picture no. 118 is seen more closely here. It was erected in 1970 to link the platforms as the demolition of the High Level station removed the only access to the up side. No. 33015 waits to return with a sandite special on 23rd November 1985, crushed leaves otherwise causing problems on this steeply graded route. (A.Dasi-Sutton)

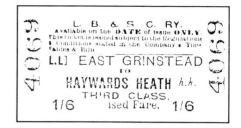

121. Until 1987, DEMUs could be berthed in the two remaining goods sidings or straight ahead, on Imberhorne Viaduct, where no. 33064 is standing on 15th May 1994 following a collision. The sign on the left announces *SITE FOR FUTURE BLUEBELL RAILWAY STATION*. The road on the left was laid down in 1992. (M.J.Stretton)

Other views of this station and the lines radiating from it are contained in the companion album
Branch Lines to East Grinstead.
The station is also included among many historic pictures in
East Grinstead Then & Now
(both from Middleton Press).

122. A northward view from the public footbridge in March 1994 includes the revised track layout for electrification, this using fewer points than a scissors crossover. The home town of Dr. Beeching then had a greatly improved train service to London than it had in the days of his influence on the railways of Britain. (M.Turvey)

MP Middleton Press

Easebourne Lane, Midhurst. West Sussex. GU29 9AZ   Tel: 01730 813169   Fax: 01730 812601

. . . . . Write or telephone for our latest list . . . . .

BRANCH LINES

Branch Line to Allhallows
Branch Lines to Alton
Branch Lines tround Ascot
Branch Line to Bude
Branch Lines to East Grinstead
Branch Lines tround Effingham Jn
Branch Lines to Exmouth
Branch Line to Fairford
Branch Lines around Gosport
Branch Line to Hawkhurst
Branch Line to Hayling
Branch Lines to Horsham
Branch Lines around Huntingdon
Branch Lines to Ilfracombe
Branch Line to Lyme Regis
Branch Line to Lynton
Branch Lines around March
Branch Lines around Midhurst
Branch Line to Minehead
Branch Lines to Newport
Branch Lines around Portmadoc 1923-46
Branch Lines around Porthmadog 1954-94
Branch Lines to Seaton & Sidmouth
Branch Line to Selsey
Branch Lines around Sheerness
Branch Line to Shrewsbury
Branch Line to Southwold
Branch Line to Swanage
Branch Line to Tenterden
Branch Lines to Torrington
Branch Lines to Tunbridge Wells
Branch Lines tround Weymouth

LONDON SUBURBAN RAILWAYS

Caterham and Tattenham Corner
Charing Cross to Dartford
Clapham Jn. to Beckenham Jn.
Crystal Palace and Catford Loop
Holborn Viaduct to Lewisham
Lewisham to Dartford
London Bridge to Addiscombe
Mitcham Junction Lines
South London Line
West Croydon to Epsom

STEAMING THROUGH

Steaming through Cornwall
Steaming through East Sussex
Steaming through the Isle of Wight
Steaming through Surrey
Steaming through West Hants
Steaming through West Sussex

SOUTH COAST RAILWAYS

Ashford to Dover
Bournemouth to Weymouth
Brighton to Eastbourne
Brighton to Worthing
Chichester to Portsmouth
Dover to Ramsgate
Hastings to Ashford
Ryde to Ventnor

SOUTHERN MAIN LINES

Bromley South to Rochester
Charing Cross to Orpington
Crawley to Littlehampton
Dartford to Sittingbourne
East Croydon to Three Bridges
Epsom to Horsham
Exeter to Barnstaple
Faversham to Dover
Haywards Heath to Seaford
London Bridge to East Croydon
Orpington to Tonbridge
Salisbury to Yeovil
Sittingbourne to Ramsgate
Swanley to Ashford
Three Bridges to Brighton
Tonbridge to Hastings
Victoria to Bromley South
Waterloo to Windsor
Waterloo to Woking
Woking to Southampton
Yeovil to Exeter

COUNTRY RAILWAY ROUTES

Andover to Southampton
Bath To Evercreech Junction
Bournemouth to Evercreech Jn
Burnham to Evercreech Junction
Croydon to East Grinstead
East Kent Light Railway
Fareham to Salisbury
Guildford to Redhill
Porthmadog to Blaenau
Reading to Basingstoke
Reading to Guildford
Redhill to Ashford
Salisbury to Westbury
Strood to Paddock Wood
Woking to Alton

SOUTHERN RAILWAY VIDEOS

Memories of the Lyme Regis Branc
War on the Line

TRAMWAY CLASSICS

Bournemouth & Poole Tramways
Brighton's Tramways
Camberwell & W. Norwood Tramwa
Croydon's Tramways
Dover's Tramways
Embankment & Waterloo Tramway
Exeter & Taunton Tramways
Greenwich & Dartford Tramways
Hastings Tramways
Lewisham & Catford Tramways
Maidstone & Chatham Tramways
North Kent Tramways
Southampton Tramways
Southend-on-sea Tramways
Thanet's Tramways
Victoria & Lambeth Tramways

BUS BOOKS

Eastbourne Bus Story
Tillingbourne Bus Story

OTHER RAILWAY BOOKS

Garraway Father & Son
Industrial Railways of the South East
London Chatham & Dover Railway
South Eastern Railway
War on the Line

MILITARY BOOKS

Battle Over Portsmouth
Battle Over Sussex 1940
Blitz Over Sussex 1941-42
Bombers over Sussex 1943-45
Military Defence of West Sussex

WATERWAY ALBUMS

Hampshire Waterways
Kent and East Sussex Waterways
London to Portsmouth Waterway
West Sussex Waterways

COUNTRY BOOKS

Brickmaking in Sussex
East Grinstead Then and Now
Leigh Park
Walking Ashdown Forest